The
Canadian Rockies
A Winter Paradise

Summerthought

Banff, Canada

THE CANADIAN ROCKIES: A WINTER PARADISE

Published by

Summerthought

Summerthought Publishing
PO Box 2309
Banff, AB T1L 1C1
Canada
www.summerthought.com

1st Edition—2008

Front cover (bound): Lake Louise, Banff National Park. Copyright © 2008 Andrew Hempstead.
Front cover (soft cover): Bow Lake, Icefields Parkway. Copyright © 2008 William Manning.

Images copyright © 2008 Craig Douce, except Richard Hallman/Sunshine Village 94; Sean Hannah/Sunshine Village 45; Andrew Hempstead 4-5, 6, 12-13, 14-15, 19, 22-23, 24, 25, 26-27, 28, 29, 30, 48, 50, 58, 64, 72, 76-77, 88, 89, 92-93; Jessica Pitt/Marmot Basin 49.

Text copyright © 2008 by Summerthought Publishing.

Design and production: Linda Petras
Printed in Canada by Friesens

Library and Archives Canada Cataloguing in Publication

Douce, Craig
The Canadian Rockies : a winter paradise / photographed by Craig Douce.

Issued in bound format, with photo of Lake Louise, Banff National Park on cover;
and in paperback format, with photo of Bow Lake, Icefields Parkway, on cover.

ISBN 978-0-9782375-7-8 (pbk.)—ISBN 978-0-9782375-8-5 (bound)

1. Rocky Mountains, Canadian (B.C. and Alta.)—Pictorial works. 2. Winter—Rocky Mountains, Canadian (B.C. and Alta.)
—Pictorial works. I. Title.

FC219.D68 2008   971.1'050222   C2008-905023-1

About the Photographer

Craig Douce is a Canmore, Alberta-based photographer whose editorial, fine art, and event images have been published by clients worldwide. Since graduating from the Southern Alberta Institute of Technology's Journalism Arts program, he has received numerous photographic awards and his photography has been exhibited in locations such as the Banff Centre, the Whyte Museum of the Canadian Rockies, and in many private collections. For more information about the photographer and his work, visit www.craigdouce.com.

Introduction

The thought of the Canadian Rockies in winter evokes images of a mountainous winter playground blanketed in snow, of abundant wildlife scattered through the wilderness, of resorts filled with skiers and snowboarders, and of grandiose mountain lodges infused with holiday cheer.

From the thrill of spotting a moose to the excitement of a backcountry ski adventure, the alluring images of local photographer of Craig Douce in *The Canadian Rockies: A Winter Paradise* will take you on a memorable journey through one of the world's most scenic landscapes.

Distinctive
Castle Mountain
is easily recognized
between Banff
and Lake Louise.

The gateway to the Canadian Rockies is Canmore, beautifully situated on the Bow River west of Calgary.

The first rays of winter sun illuminate trees along the Bow River (opposite).

Policeman's Creek,
Canmore.

Mount Assiniboine.

Kananaskis River, Kananaskis Country.

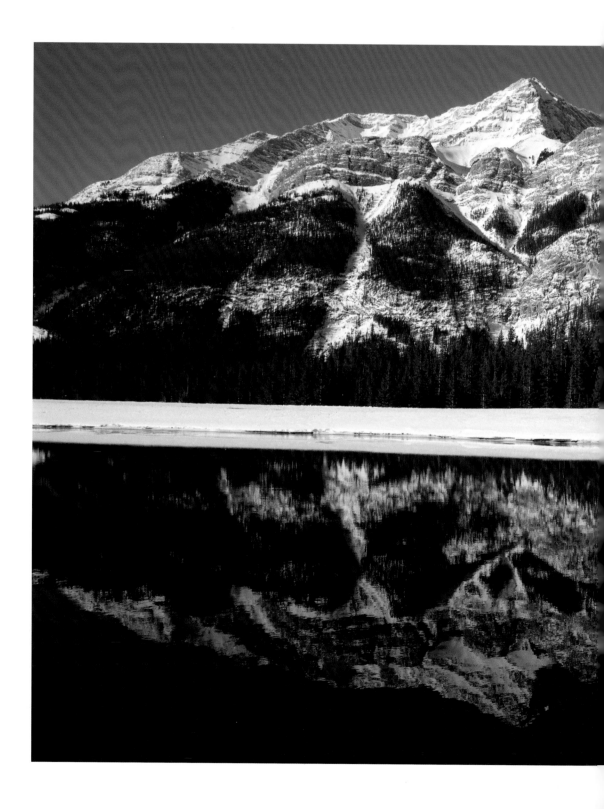

Spray Lakes
Provincial Park,
Kananaskis Country.

The Fairmont
Banff Springs
is one of the
world's grandest
mountain resorts.

Looking down to the town of Banff
from Mount Norquay Road.

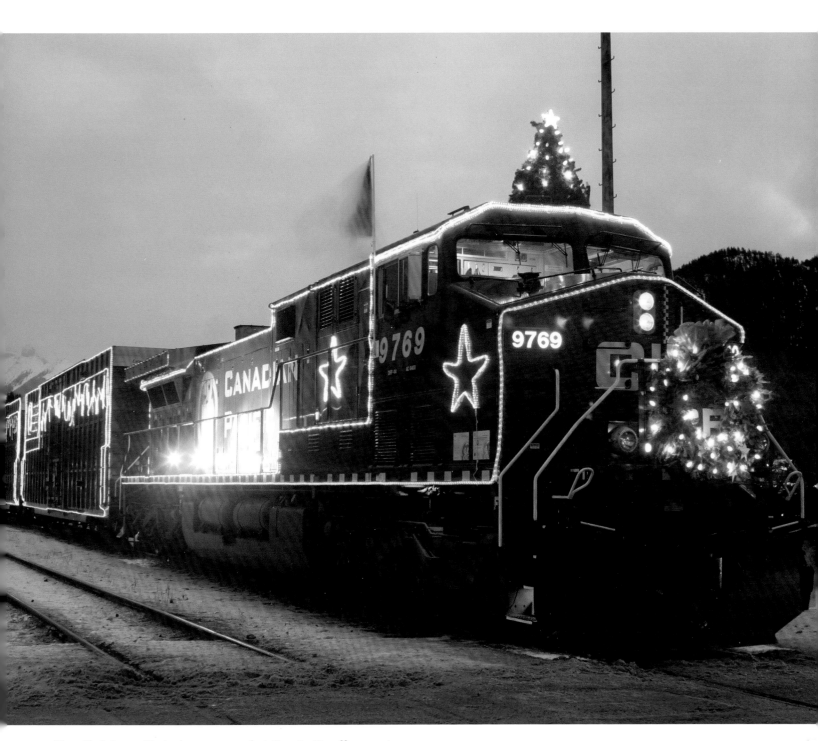

The Christmas Train is an annual visitor to Banff.

Solitude along the road to Lake Minnewanka.

Storm clouds often gather around the summit of Mount Rundle, which can be seen from downtown Banff (opposite).

Sunrise over Storm Mountain, which straddles the Continental Divide and forms the boundary between Banff and Kootenay National Parks.

A skating rink in
front of the Fairmont
Chateau Lake Louise
is surely one of the
world's most scenic.

At higher elevations along the Icefields Parkway, trees stunted by the harsh climate poke above the snow.

In winter, the Columbia Icefield is a stark, desolate landscape where travellers can imagine what the region looked like during the last ice age.

The Icefields Parkway, linking Banff and Jasper National Parks, is a spectacular drive at any time of year, but in winter extra precautions must be taken as there are no services en route.

Weeping Wall,
Icefields Parkway.

Sunrise over a partially frozen Athabasca River, Jasper National Park.

Heavy snowfalls are part of everyday life in the Canadian Rockies.

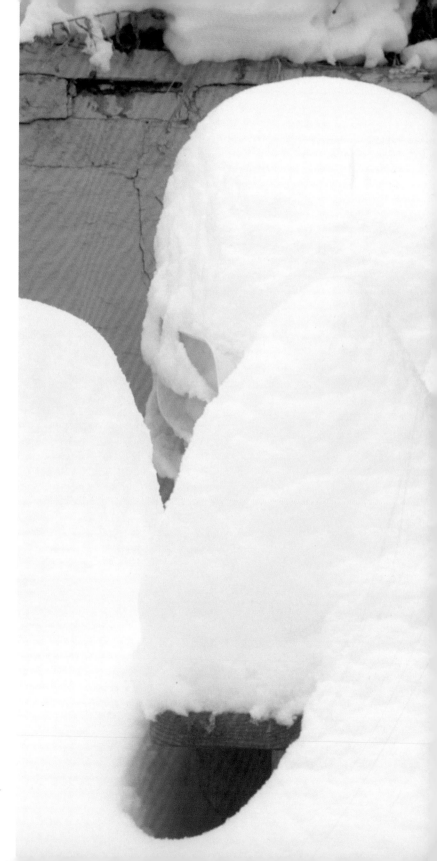

For local children, heavy snowfalls are a way of life.

Coyotes crossing a frozen lake.

Bighorn sheep.

An elk, seemingly buried to her neck in a snowdrift.

Moose are the largest of the hoofed mammals present in the Canadian Rockies.

Ducks remain year-round in the Canadian Rockies, finding watery playgrounds that don't freeze, such as this one on Canmore's Policeman's Creek.

Hot springs flowing into Vermilion Lakes allow birds such as this dipper to remain in the Canadian Rockies through winter.

Winter storms make driving
especially challenging.

Expert skiers and snowboarders
relish "powder days" in the
Canadian Rockies.

Sunshine Village is accessible only by gondola from the valley floor.

Natural snow is supplemented by manmade snow, which is made by forcing water and air through "snow cannons" when the temperature is below freezing.

Nakiska, in Kananaskis Country, was developed for the downhill events of the 1988 Winter Olympic Games.

A perfect day for skiing and boarding at Marmot Basin, in Jasper National Park (opposite).

Lake Louise is one of Canada's largest winter resorts.

Jan Hudec (opposite, competing in a World Cup race at Lake Louise)
is one of many champions who have honed their skills on local ski hills.

Terrain parks allow skiers and snowboarders to jump, spin, and twist across manmade obstacles day and night (opposite).

Snowboard competitions are held in terrain parks (left) while racing (opposite) is known as boardercross.

Avalanches (opposite) are a constant concern in the
backcountry. Visitors minimize their chances of disaster
by checking conditions at local visitor centres and
taking note of signage.

Cross-country skiing is a popular
recreational activity throughout the
Canadian Rockies.

Established for
the 1988 Winter
Olympic Games,
the Canmore
Nordic Centre still
hosts cross-country
ski races, but is also
open to the public
for recreational
skiing.

The Canadian Rockies provide a home for many world-class winter athletes, including Sara Renner (opposite) and Chandra Crawford (above), both seen here competing at the Canmore Nordic Centre.

Snowshoeing toward
Talon Peak, a remote
backcountry destination on
the British Columbia side of
the Canadian Rockies.

Frozen lakes, such as Cascade Ponds near the town of Banff, create an ideal venue for locals to play ice hockey, which in Canada is simply known as "hockey."

Children take up winter sports at a young age in the Canadian Rockies.

Learning to skate.

A young hockey
player hones
his skills on an
outdoor rink.

Watch hockey stars of the future at home games of the Canmore Eagles, who play throughout the winter months at the Canmore Recreation Centre.

Locals enjoying
"pond hockey" on
Lake Louise.

The Canmore Ice Climbing Festival draws experienced climbers away from the mountains to showcase their skills in downtown Canmore.

An ice-climber takes
advantage of the
last rays of sunlight.

Dogsledding, also known as "mushing," is a traditional form of transportation that visitors can enjoy themselves at a slow pace, or they can watch the excitement of racing (pictured).

Competitive ski jumping at Ski Norquay, Banff National Park.

Ice fishing on
Spray Lake,
Kananaskis Country.

83

It's not all fun and games in the mountains, as these brave folks practice rescue techniques in icy water.

Snowshoers
make their way
toward the
Fairmont Chateau
Lake Louise,
one of many
upscale resorts
scattered through
the Canadian
Rockies.

Num-Ti-Jah Lodge, along the Icefields Parkway, is a charming log lodge with a colourful history.

Adirondack chairs brighten the scene at Fairmont Jasper Park Lodge (opposite).

89

The
Santa Claus Parade
is a Christmas
tradition in Banff.

During Ice Magic,
at Lake Louise, blocks of ice
are transformed into intricate
works of art.

Hot pools throughout the Canadian Rockies provide a soothing end to a day of outdoor recreation. Pictured is Sunshine Village (right) and Banff's Upper Hot Springs (opposite).

The Slush Cup, with skiers and snowboarders attempting to glide gracefully across a pool of very cold water in fancy costumes (or nothing at all, as pictured), signifies the end of winter at Sunshine Village.